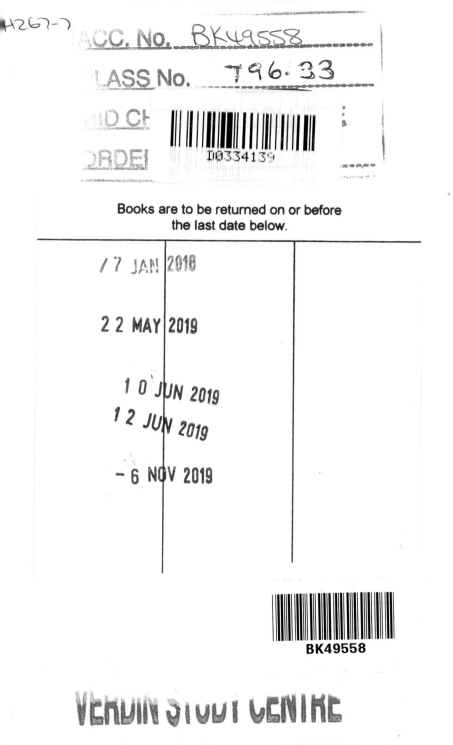

First published in 2007 in Great Britain by
Barrington Stoke Ltd
18 Walker St, Edinburgh, EH3 7LP

www.barringtonstoke.co.uk

Reprinted 2008

ISBN: 978-1-84299-512-9

Printed in Great Britain by Bell & Bain Ltd

A Note from the Author

You don't hear much racist abuse at football games these days. Thank goodness. At least not in the Premiership. But black players used to get it all the time. It was horrible. It still happens when England play away games.

I don't know how some players put up with it. But I have always admired those who did. The best players showed the stupid racists what they think of them by playing well.

Sol Campbell has always been one of those players. I am not a Spurs fan, an Arsenal fan or a Portsmouth fan. But I have always been a fan of Sol Campbell.

For Pauline, Trevor and Will,
loyal Pompey fans

Contents

Chapter 1

The Rock

Sol Campbell is one of the best ever footballers of our time.

He is strong in the air. He is fast on the ball. He has two good feet. He reads the game. He times his tackles well. He works hard. He rules the defence.

To other teams, Sol Campbell is fast as an eagle and scary as a tiger. His team-mates say he is as gentle as a giant, but solid as a rock.

This is the story of the poor boy from the East End of London who grew up to be captain of Spurs, Arsenal and England.

It's a story of skill and guts, hard work, hard luck and winning.

It is the story of Sol Campbell. The Rock.

Chapter 2

Kick Off

Sol Campbell was born in London on 18 September 1974. His full name is Sulzeer Jeremiah Campbell. That's a bit hard to say. So his family just called him Sol.

His parents were born in Jamaica. After they came to England, they lived in a small

three-bedroom house in Stratford, in the East
End of London. Sol's dad worked on the
railways. His mum worked in a car factory.

Life was hard. They didn't have much
money. And they didn't have much room.
Sol had nine older brothers and two sisters.
That's right – there were 12 children! That's
six kids in each bedroom.

The East End of London is a hard place to
grow up. Most of all if you're black. Sol had

to be strong. He had to win respect.

Sol learned to look after himself. People said he was shy. But he just liked being quiet. He also learned to chill. (It's his favourite word, chill.)

Sol went to Lister Community School. Soon he started playing football. He was good. Very good. In those days Sol played in mid-field. He was picked to play for Essex Boys. In the same team was a boy called David Beckham.

West Ham was his favourite team in those days. But when Sol was 13, a scout from Spurs saw him playing. Spurs asked Sol to train with their youth team.

At first Sol didn't think he was that good. But soon he was going to White Hart Lane to train after school. It took him one and a half hours to get there by bus and tube. And another hour and a half to get home. It was hard, but Sol was used to things being hard.

Spurs knew that Sol was good. But they didn't know where to play him. At times he played as a defender. Other times he played in mid-field. He even played as a striker.

Sol was so good he was asked to go to a new school run by the FA School at Lilleshall. It was in the country. Young Sol had never seen so many fields before. He was one of the first young players to attend. While he was there he met a young boy called Michael Owen.

In 1993 Sol was in the Under-18 England squad. Paul Scholes, Robbie Fowler and Gary Neville were also in that team. Together

they won the Under-18 European

Championship.

One day they would all play together for

England.

Chapter 3

White Hart Lane

In 1992 Spurs gave Sol a three-year contract. A few weeks later he came on as a sub against Chelsea. Spurs lost the game, but Sol scored. He didn't play again that season. Played 1, goals 1. That's not a bad record for a defender.

The next season he played 34 games for Spurs. Soon Sol was Tottenham's best defender. He was made club captain. All the Spurs fans loved Sol. He was their hero.

In 1999 Sol was captain of Spurs when they won against Leicester City in the League Cup final. With Sol at the back, Spurs reached the FA Cup semi-final three times. But they couldn't get to the final.

Tottenham Hotspur always played good football. They liked to please the crowd. But it was a long time since they had won any

major prizes. The club seemed to be stuck in the middle of the table. And they were always sacking their managers. Sol played under 10 managers in eight years. He decided it was time to move on.

In 2001, Sol's contract came to an end. So he could leave Spurs if he wanted.

Sol loved Spurs. He had been with them since he was 14. In eight seasons he played 315 games for the club and scored 15 goals. But Sol wanted to win more cups.

Everyone said Sol was the best defender in the country. Lots of big clubs in Italy, Germany and Spain wanted Sol. He could have gone to any club in the world if he wanted. It was hard to decide.

Some people said he would go to Bayern Munich. Some people said he would choose Inter Milan. Most people said he would play for Barcelona. No one said he would move to Arsenal ...

Arsenal are Tottenham's biggest rivals. Spurs fans hate Arsenal. Sol Campbell was

their captain and their hero. He couldn't go to Arsenal – could he?

Spurs fans were angry and upset when they heard the news. Some fans even said they would kill him. They called him a traitor and a 'Judas'. But Sol was cool. He just got on with playing football. He knew he was the best. He knew how to chill.

Chapter 4
Three Lions

It wasn't long before Sol was picked to play for his country. His first game for England was in May 1996 against Hungary. Manager Terry Venables picked him for the England squad for Euro 1996.

He played next to Tony Adams in the middle of the defence. When Tony Adams retired from international football Sol was the best person to replace him.

Sol helped England reach the 1998 World Cup finals in France. He helped England reach Euro 2000. He played in all the group games.

The England manager Sven-Goran Erikson made Sol captain in his first game in charge when David Beckham came off the pitch. In the 2002 World Cup, Sol and Rio Ferdinand

were fantastic at the back. Sol scored an amazing goal against Sweden. He was brilliant against Argentina.

FIFA named Sol in their World Cup All-Star squads for 1998 and 2002. UEFA voted him the best English player of Euro 2004.

But Sol was hurt in 2005. While he was getting better, his place in the England team was taken by John Terry. Sol was back in the squad for the 2006 World Cup in Germany. But Sven didn't play him in the team. The new England manager Steve McClaren didn't

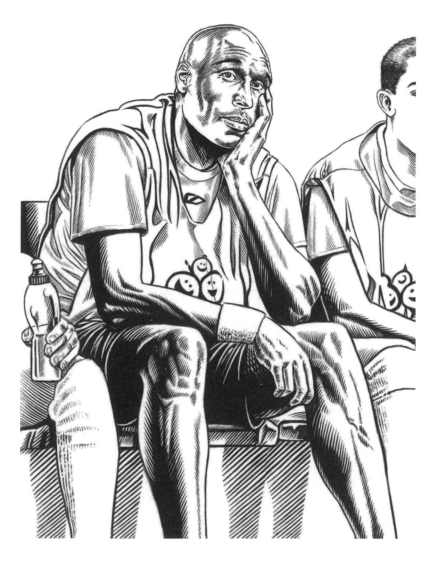

even pick him for his first squad. He wanted younger players.

After 69 games for his country, Sol's England career was over. He had captained England three times. He is the only player ever to play for England in six major competitions. Sol Campbell is still one of the most-capped England players of all time.

Chapter 5

The Gunners

When Sol joined Arsenal they had lots of brilliant players like Thierry Henri, Patrick Vieira and Tony Adams.

Sol made his debut for Arsenal in August 2000, against Middlesbrough. Arsenal won 4–0.

Sol played next to Tony Adams in the middle of the Arsenal defence. When Tony Adams hung up his boots, Sol became the club's main central defender. Just like in the England team.

In his first season at Highbury, Sol played 48 games. The next season he played 43 games. The season after that he played 44 games. Manager Arsène Wenger said that Sol was the 'back-bone' of his team.

Sol is 188 cm tall. He weighs 90 kg. Not many players get past Sol Campbell. Thierry

Henri helped score the goals. Sol Campbell helped keep them out.

In 2003–4 Arsenal didn't lose a single league game all season. No team had done this for over 100 years! With Sol at the back, the team only let in 26 goals. They went 49 games without losing. This was another new English record.

In 2002 Arsenal won the League and Cup double. In 2004 they won the League again.

The FA picked Sol for the Premiership team of the season. Arsenal were FA Cup winners again in 2003 and 2005.

The following year Sol was hurt. When he came back into the team he started making mistakes. He tried hard. He trained hard. But something wasn't right. Then he suddenly vanished for several days. No one knew where he had gone. Arsenal couldn't find him. The press couldn't find him. What was he doing? No one knows. But perhaps Sol just needed to chill.

He came back after a few days. He was soon back in the Arsenal team. But he broke his nose in his first game and needed an operation.

A few weeks later, Sol helped Arsenal beat Villarreal in the semi-final of the Champions League. In the final they had to play the great Barcelona. Sol was brilliant. He even scored with a header. But Barcelona won the game 2–1.

Chapter 6

Unlucky

Sol Campbell has done very well. But he has also had a lot of bad luck.

Sol's first game for England was against Ireland in 1995. The match was stopped because of crowd trouble. So Sol didn't win his first cap. Unlucky.

In the 1998 World Cup, England were drawing 2–2 with Argentina. England were down to 10 men. There were only 10 minutes left, when Sol headed the ball over the line.

Goal! England were through. Sol ran to the corner to celebrate. But the ref had blown for a foul by Alan Shearer. The goal was not allowed. Argentina won on penalties and England were out of the World Cup. Unlucky.

In 2003 Sol was sent off against Man United. The ref thought Sol hit Solskjaer

with his arm. Sol was suspended for three
games. He missed the FA Cup Final.
Unlucky.

In Euro 2004 England met Portugal in the
quarter-final. The score was 1–1. In the last
minute Sol headed the ball over the line.
Goal! England were through. But the ref had
blown for a foul by John Terry. The goal was
not allowed. Portugal won on penalties and
England were out again. Unlucky.

When Arsenal went to Old Trafford in
2005 they were 11 points clear at the top. At

the time no one could beat Arsenal. But with 18 minutes to go Wayne Rooney ran into the box. Sol stretched out his leg to tackle him. Rooney went down. Penalty! United won the game. Arsenal's unbeaten record was broken. So was their confidence. Arsenal lost the title. Unlucky.

Later that year Arsenal played Man United in the FA Cup Final. This time Arsenal won. But Sol was hurt, so he missed the game. Unlucky.

Sol Campbell has had a lot of bad luck. But he always stays cool. He knows he is the best. Sol knows how to chill.

Chapter 7

Pompey

Sol played 197 games for Arsenal. While he was there they won the Premier League twice and the FA Cup three times. He was part of the best Arsenal team ever.

But after five seasons at Highbury the Gunners let him go. Where would Sol go next? Everyone thought he would play for a team in Europe. But Sol went to Portsmouth.

Lots of people thought Sol was crazy. Pompey were almost relegated the year before. But Sol wanted a new challenge. And he had lots of friends at Portsmouth. His old England mates David James and Andy Cole were there. Kanu used to play with Sol at Arsenal. So did Portsmouth's assistant manager Tony Adams.

Portsmouth manager Harry Rednapp organised the team around Sol. With Sol at the back they had one of the strongest defences in the Premier League. After five games Portsmouth were top.

Manager Harry Rednapp built the team round Sol. With Sol and Linvoy Primus at the back, Portsmouth had one of the strongest defences in the Premier League. They kept 12 clean sheets.

Sol played in nearly every game. He even scored a goal, against Sheffield Utd. After five games Portsmouth were top. At the end of the season they were 9th, just two points outside a place in the UEFA Cup.

Play up Pompey!

Nice one Sol.

Chapter 8

Sol Man

Today Sol is a millionaire. He owns a two million pound house. He used to drive a Porsche with the number plate SOL 1. He wears very expensive clothes. Sometimes he flies out to Italy, just to buy clothes!

Sol has had lots of celebrity girlfriends, like pop singer Dido, tennis star Martina Hingis, designer Kelly Hoppen, model Gabrielle Richens and R&B singer Christina Milian. He has even starred in Footballer's Wives. He has a son called Joseph.

He is so famous that his name is now used in Cockney rhyming slang. If you say, "I'm going for a Sol", it means you are "going for a Sol Campbell". Campbell rhymes with 'ramble', which is another word for a walk. So if you say you are "going for a Sol", it means you are going for a walk!

Sol raises a lot of money for good causes, mostly children's charities. Sol was one of the sports stars who helped London bid for the 2012 Olympics. Many of the new Olympic sports grounds will be in the East End of London where Sol grew up.

Sol also likes reading. "Training keeps your body fit," he says, "reading keeps you mentally fit."

Sol still works hard to stay fit. Before every game he eats the same meal of rice,

fish, yoghurt and water. He eats lots of pasta. Sometimes he even has pasta for breakfast. And he really likes spinach too – just like Popeye.

Sol supports Kick Racism Out of Football and Show Racism the Red Card. He hates racism anywhere, not only on the football pitch.

He says that no one should abuse another human being because of their colour. "It's out of order." He thinks football should bring people together. "It's great to see a good mix of people enjoying football. That's why I love being part of it."

Sol is now over 30. What will he do when he retires from football? Perhaps he will become a manager. Perhaps he will start his own fashion label. Or maybe he will become a Hollywood actor. He says he wants to travel. He is learning to speak French.

Whatever he does, Sol Campbell will do it well. He won't cause a fuss. After all, his favourite word is still 'chill'.

Barrington Stoke would like to thank all its readers for commenting on the manuscript before publication and in particular:

Mohammed Al-Dossary

Lewis Bourne

Daniel Brown

Lynne Brown

Ryan Elliot

Connor Henderson

Madeleine Knight

Gillian McMultan

Kyle Page

Colin Randall

Gazza Richardson

Lewis Spencer

Kerry Stephenson

Kristina Walters

Become a Consultant!

Would you like to give us feedback on our titles before they are published? Contact us at the email address below – we'd love to hear from you!

info@barringtonstoke.co.uk
www.barringtonstoke.co.uk

Great reads – no problem!

Barrington Stoke books are:

Great stories – from thrillers to comedy to horror, and all by the best writers around!

No hassle – fast reads with no boring bits, and a story that doesn't let go of you till the last page.

Short – the perfect size for a fast, fun read.

We use our own font and paper to make it easier to read our books. And we ask teenagers like you, who want a no-hassle read, to check every book before it's published.

That way, we know for sure that every Barrington Stoke book is a great read for everyone.

Check out www.barringtonstoke.co.uk for more info about Barrington Stoke and our books!

If you loved this book

why don't you read ...

Death Leap
by Simon Chapman

Jake saw a murder
The killers saw Jake
Now the killers are after him ...

gr8reads

If you loved this book

why don't you read ...

Kiss of Death
by Charles Butler

Kate wants Nick
Nothing will stop her.
Not even *death* ...

gr8reads

If you loved this book why don't you read ...

Gremlin
by Chris Powling

The pilot is sick.
The plane will crash.
Can Glenn save it?

gr8reads

If you loved this book
why don't you read …

Thing
by Chris Powling

Black button eyes
Zig-zag mouth
Stiff body
Thing
Once it was Robbie's best friend
Now it's become his enemy …

You can order *Thing* directly from our website at
www.barringtonstoke.co.uk